Dedic

Sweet Camille

As you continue your journey in life with learning, laughter and love, thank you for including us in the joy and magic of seeing the world (once again!) through the eyes of a child.

We love making memories with you and by doing so, we will always be with you.

Love

Grammy and Poppy

Est. 2017

Hello Again!

My name is Camille, and this is my second "How To" book. I just learned how to use the potty. I started on a little potty that my Mom and Dad took EVERYWHERE we went! Being able to use the potty is one of the skills you need to master before learning to wipe your bottom.

LITTLE POTTY

Once I learned to use the big potty my Mom and Dad thought the next step was learning to wipe my bottom.

BIG POTTY

But Wait...

Learning to wipe your bottom takes
DEX-TER-ITY!

That's a big word for having the skills and ability to reach and wipe your bottom!

So...

If your Mom or Dad think you're ready...

Let's learn together!

It only takes toilet paper and a lot of practice!

There are many different names for what we call our bottoms. Some of these are heinie, butt, backside, tushie, rear-end or fanny.

No matter what you call it... it's very important to keep it clean!

My Grammy says it is always helpful to use the problem-solving method to learn a skill by asking the questions

WHO?
WHAT?
WHERE?
WHEN?

(and most importantly)

HOW?

Let's start at the beginning!

WHO?

People are the only ones that wipe their bottoms after going to the potty. This is because we are called BIPEDS (which means we walk on 2 legs) and need to clean the area covered up by our heinie cheeks.

WHAT?

We are learning how to wipe your bottom. You use 2 parts of your body to wipe your bottom.

Can you point to the child's hands and bottom?

MY BODY

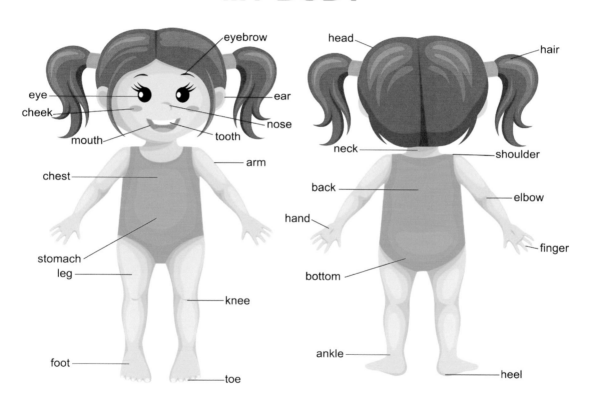

eyebrow

eye

cheek

mouth

ear

nose

tooth

arm

chest

stomach

leg

knee

foot

toe

head

hair

neck

shoulder

back

elbow

hand

finger

bottom

ankle

heel

WHERE?

You can wipe your bottom anywhere because it is part of your body and you always have it with you.

The only other things you need is a potty, toilet paper and...

... a sink to wash your hands.

WHEN?

You wipe your bottom EVERY TIME you poop in the potty. Sometimes it will be stinky and messy to clean up.

That makes it even more important to know how to keep your bottom clean!

HOW?

1. Make sure you're done pooping before you start to wipe.

2. Take 3 pieces of toilet paper and fold in half and half again.

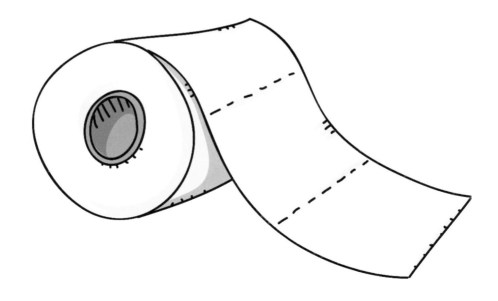

SPECIAL NOTE TO PARENTS:

When learning to wipe many parents find flushable wipes an easier and cleaner method.

Flushable wipes are a good teaching tool but should be disposed of properly!

3. Place the toilet paper in your preferred hand PALM SIDE UP.

   Your preferred hand is the one you use to eat, brush your teeth, wave, color, and the one you use to wipe your bottom.

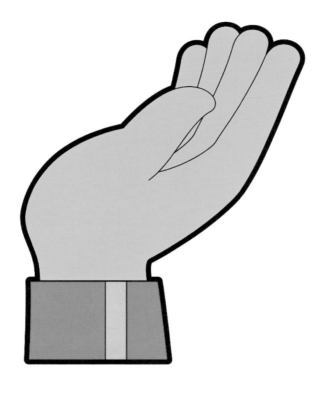

The toilet paper pad should cover your fingers but not your thumb.

4. Lean forward or sideways lifting part of your bottom off the seat.

5. Wipe front to back or side to side with the toilet paper pad.
6. Use a new toilet paper pad for EACH wipe. Look at the toilet paper pad each time you wipe before you throw it in the toilet.
7. Wipe at least 2 times to make sure your bottom is clean.
8. WIPE TILL YOU SEE WHITE and there is no more poop on the paper.

9. Get off the potty and pull up your pants.

10. Flush the toilet. Have Mom or
    Dad show you how to flush.

WASH YOUR HANDS

GREAT JOB! YOU'RE ALL DONE!

WOW!

That's a lot of steps to learn. Let's practice off the toilet sitting on a chair with your clothes on.

1. Practice making toilet paper pads with 3 sheets of toilet paper. Fold in half and half again.

2. Put the pre-folded sheets in a plastic container to have ready when you need them.

   This will prevent pulling too much toilet paper from the roll while you are first learning to wipe your bottom.

3. Have Mom or Dad sit on a chair and show you each of the steps to wipe your bottom.

Watch closely and then YOU try each step just like they showed you.

4. Practice bending forward and sideways and see which is the easiest for you to reach your bottom.

Make sure you lift your bottom off the toilet seat.

5. Practice wiping (front to back if leaning forward or side to side if leaning sideways). Always look at the toilet paper pad each time you wipe to make sure your bottom is clean.

6. Keep practicing with Mom or Dad to learn all the steps and you'll be wiping your bottom like a CHAMP!

We have so much more to learn

LET'S DO IT TOGETHER!

ACKNOWLEDGEMENTS

Any success we have in life should be shared with those who through their love, friendship, support, time, and talent help you achieve great things. My second children's "How To" book is no exception. Those special people in my life who contributed to my first book remain unchanged and I offer my heartfelt thanks and gratitude.

Note from Author

This is my second "How To" book written for my granddaughter, Camille. Based on my 25 years of experience working in the training and curriculum development for individuals with intellectual disabilities these "How To" books apply to all learners. Topics are chosen by where Camille is developmentally and as she grows, I will have endless opportunities (and ideas) to follow her journey as a lifelong learner. My beloved husband Don (aka Poppy) has encouraged me to stop before attempting to write, "How to Parallel Park" as I have not mastered the skill in my 69 years AND at this rate will be 83 when Camille is ready for her driving test! There is so much to teach/learn with our young loved ones, I invite you to join me on this journey.

Best Wishes
Cindy Yard (aka Grammy Yard)

WATCH FOR MORE OF MY BOOKS IN THE FUTURE!

Made in United States
Troutdale, OR
01/02/2025

27531345R00031